PUB W...
l
Lincolnshire

Brett Collier

COUNTRYSIDE BOOKS
NEWBURY BERKSHIRE

COUNTRYSIDE BOOKS
3 Catherine Road
Newbury, Berkshire

To view our complete range of books,
please visit us at
www.countrysidebooks.co.uk

ISBN 978 1 84674 048 0

Cover picture of the Lincolnshire Wolds
supplied by Bill Meadows

Designed by Peter Davies, Nautilus Design
Typeset by Jean Cussons Typesetting, Diss, Norfolk
Produced through MRM Associates Ltd., Reading
Printed by Cambridge University Press

Contents

AREA MAP SHOWING LOCATION OF THE WALKS

Walk

PUBLISHER'S NOTE

We hope that you obtain considerable enjoyment from this book; great care has been taken in its preparation. However, changes of landlord and actual closures of pubs are sadly not uncommon. Likewise, although at the time of publication all routes followed public rights of way or permitted paths, diversion orders can be made and permissions withdrawn.

We cannot, of course, be held responsible for such diversion orders and any inaccuracies in the text which result from these or any other changes to the routes nor any damage which might result from walkers trespassing on private property. We are anxious though that all details covering the walks are kept up to date and would therefore welcome information from readers which would be relevant to future editions.

The simple sketch maps that accompany the walks in this book are based on notes made by the author whilst checking out the routes on the ground. However, for the benefit of a proper map, we do recommend that you purchase the relevant Ordnance Survey sheet covering your walk. The Ordnance Survey maps are widely available, especially through booksellers and local newsagents.

INTRODUCTION

This book covers the sparsely populated 'old Lincolnshire', from the Humber to the Wash. The pace of life can be slow here and there are miles and miles of empty field paths waiting to be explored, with lots of space under wide horizons, be it farmland, heathland, wold, fen, or salt marsh. Lincolnshire is supposed not to have any scenery at all and has been said to be dull, flat and uninteresting. However, you will find for yourself that the very size of the county means that there is a range of scenery and geographical features difficult to match elsewhere in lowland Britain.

There are also welcoming pubs to be discovered in villages with incredible names such as Anton's Gowt, Barnoldby le Beck, Burton upon Stather, Gedney Drove End, and many more. During your walks and explorations, you will find that the Romans were here, followed by the Vikings and each of them left their mark upon roads, dykes, villages and towns. In the Second World War, Lincolnshire became 'Bomber County' and even today OS maps show the outline of many a wartime airfield and there is still plenty of evidence on the ground of the influence of the RAF upon the county. The effect of the Beeching destruction of rural railway routes may also be seen only too clearly in the sketch maps of some of the walks.

As a result of the relaxation of licensing laws, pubs no longer keep traditional opening hours and, therefore, I have indicated for each pub its normal pattern of opening, although some may keep different times for summer and winter. Meals are usually available from 12 noon until 2 pm, with 7 pm until 10 pm for evening meals, but some pubs have one day a week off when no meals are served. Many establishments now offer a 'traditional Sunday lunch' as a set meal on that day and may be unable to cope with bar snacks at the same time. It is wise to book meals in advance, certainly on Sundays and, in some cases, at any time over a weekend. The telephone number for each pub is given.

Most landlords have readily agreed that customers may leave their cars in the pub car park while they are doing the walk but it is only polite to warn the publican concerned that you are doing so. A strange car left in an empty car park outside normal opening hours could easily be treated with suspicion. A note left at the pub indicating your intention of returning to partake of their hospitality will certainly help to establish a good relationship. Further, as you are likely to be away some time, it is only courteous not to park immediately outside the main entrance.

The sketch maps, while perfectly adequate for each walk, cannot give you a full picture of the surrounding countryside and an OS map of the area will greatly add to your enjoyment and understanding of the countryside.

Changing out of walking boots, especially if they are muddy, is appreciated, for many country pubs are carpeted throughout nowadays. Dogs are sometimes permitted indoors but the majority of publicans are bound by hygiene regulations, which state that animals should not be present when food is being served.

The aim of the book is for you to enjoy Lincolnshire. In conclusion, I hope that it will bring you hours of good walking, for not only do the many miles of walks open up little-frequented countryside, but they also introduce you to the high quality of food and drink that is on offer.

Brett Collier

POSTSCRIPT

Sadly, Brett Collier died in 2005, but it has been my pleasure to update these walks on his behalf. As long-standing friends, Brett and I shared many happy hours exploring the Lincolnshire countryside. It is my hope that this new edition of his book will help preserve his legendary dedication to the 'byways' of our county and enable many more people to experience the many pleasures afforded by his work.

I trust it will enhance people's enjoyment to know that they will be travelling in the footsteps of a very special person whose radiant spirit lights up these pages. Please think of him kindly as you traverse these routes. Who knows, he might just be loitering around some ancient corner!

Jim Poole

The Hare and Hounds

T HIS DELIGHTFUL WALK TAKES YOU THROUGH THE VILLAGE OF GREATFORD, ACROSS THE SHILLINGTHORPE ESTATE, AND ALONGSIDE THE INFANT WEST GLEN RIVER.

Greatford, once famous for its watercress beds, is one of the most beautiful of South Kesteven's stone-built villages, with its attractive houses, unusual stone ornaments, splendid Elizabethan manor house, lovely church and small river. Kesteven existed long before the Domesday Book, as a division of the shire when the kings of Wessex won back the Danelaw. The heathland region lying to the north of Stamford reaching up to Lincoln was heavily wooded and the name 'Kesteven' derives from 'ced' or 'coed' (Celtic for wood) and 'stefna' (Scandinavian for a meeting place).

THE HARE AND HOUNDS, which dates back to the 1740s, has a stone-built fireplace in the lounge, with a huge barrel-shaped front. The walls are lined with attractive oil and water-colour paintings, offered for sale by a local artist.

The pub aims to provide a warm, friendly atmosphere for the local community and visitors alike. It succeeds very well. Good, mostly home-cooked meals are available, with dishes such as steak and ale pie and chilli con carne amongst some of the abiding favourites. Evening meals may include gammon steaks and a selection of fish dishes, such as salmon, scampi and plaice. Local game is a speciality. The sweets range from spotted dick with custard to home-made ice-cream. Well-kept beers on handpump include Wells Eagle, Wells Bombardier, Adnams Broadside and Oakham JHB. Kronenbourg and Fosters are the lagers available. There are picnic tables around the garden, with plenty of space for children to play.

The pub is open Tuesday to Saturday from 12 noon to 3 pm and from 6 pm to 11 pm; Sunday 12 noon to 3 pm. It is closed Sunday evening and all day Monday.

✆ 01778 560332.

How to get there: From the A6121 near Carlby, turn eastwards to Greatford, which is 5 miles from both Stamford and Bourne, or from the A15 Market Deeping to Bourne road, turn westwards across King Street (the Roman road) either at Baston or Langtoft.

Parking: A large car park is available at the pub for patrons but please let the landlord know you are leaving your car whilst you walk. Alternatively, limited roadside parking may be found in the village.

Length of the walk: 2¼ miles or 4½ miles. Map: OS Landranger 130 Grantham and surrounding area (GR 086118)

THE WALK

1 Turn left out of the pub for a few yards and then turn right across the bridge along the track leading to the church, with the attractive gardens and buildings of Greatford Hall on the left. After looking at the interesting church memorials and some of the inscriptions on the gravestones, turn right past the church tower and go through the graveyard to the narrow path leading down to the West Glen river and on to the lane. Turn right at the lane, over the bridge, and continue to the junction with Main Street and the old school building on the left.

2 Cross Main Street to the Old Forge, turn right for 20 yards and then left along the signposted concrete path. Continue ahead past the farm buildings, crossing a stile en route, to the fence corner on your right with a waymark. Bear slightly left across the corner of the grass field for just 84 yards to the stile and gates. Cross the stile and, with your back to it, go straight ahead on a headland path between two large arable fields, aiming for the prominent tree to the left of Barholm church.

3 Cross the narrow metal bridge over a very wide drain and over the stile. Proceed ahead over the next field along the curved headland path towards the church. Cross the track leading to the buildings of Manor Farm over on your right and continue forward towards Barholm church, with the hedge on your immediate left and a fence on your right. Climb the stone stile, with the churchyard on your right, to turn right up the lane and follow the bends round, with Manor Farm on your right. Turn to the right along the quiet lane and continue for 700 yards to the T-junction into Greatford village, with traces of ridge and furrow ploughing on your right. Note the unusual 'The Steading' sign at the edge of the garden on your left.

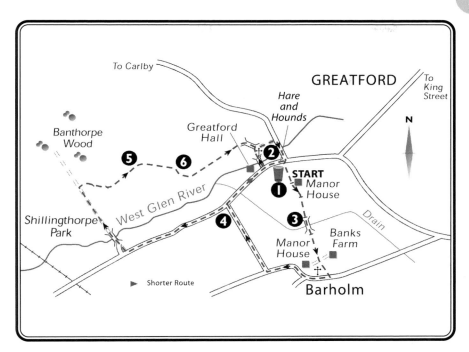

4 For the shorter walk: Turn right at the T-junction and walk along the road for ½ mile back into the village and the car park.

For the longer walk: Turn left instead of right at the T-junction and continue for nearly ¾ mile. At the entrance to Shillingthorpe Park Estate, turn right up the drive on the signposted path, with a stile at the side of the gate. Cross the bridge over the infant river and continue ahead over the next field to a copse with a metal gate. Some 157 yards beyond the gate, at the metal signpost, turn right to the stile and cross the small paddock diagonally right to another stile. Cross the next field on a slightly leftward line between the two large trees on your immediate left and the two old trees further out in the field. Pass to the left of them and aim for the summit of the rise in the following field.

5   At the earth bridge over the dyke, walk diagonally right to the far corner of the field to the small pond on your immediate right, aiming for the obvious gap in the trees on the skyline. Walk ahead past the pond to the field corner and pass through the narrow tree belt to the start of the next field.

6   After some 22 yards, turn right at the metal footpath sign on the headland path alongside the trees and ditch on your right for 155 yards to the field corner and stile. Cross the stile to enter the perimeter of the wood, bear left for 22 yards, then turn left on the path alongside the wire fence and ditch. At the first bridge with a locked gate on your right, continue ahead, then shortly, at the next bridge, turn right to cross over and walk ahead along the edge of a garden with a concrete fence on your right for 100 yards. At the end of the fence, with the iron gates of the Greatford Estate boundary on your right, turn left down the gravel drive past the house on your left and continue ahead at the tarmac section to the road. Upon reaching the road, turn right into the village to follow your original route into Main Street and back to the car park.

The Waterton Arms

THIS SURPRISINGLY VARIED WALK IS FULL OF INTEREST AND IS IDEAL FOR ANYONE WHO IS AT ALL INTERESTED IN RIVERS, WATER BIRDS OR CHURCHES. IT IS AN EASY STROLL BY THE RIVER WELLAND, ALONG THE UNUSUAL, QUIET, BACK LANE, AND WITH A MARVELLOUS 850-YEAR-OLD PRIORY CHURCH TO VISIT.

THE WATERTON ARMS is an attractive pub, named after a local family. It was built in 1600, with stone additions around 1800. There is an L-shaped bar, with low beams, plain scrubbed tables, tile and flagged floors, a restaurant area, a public bar and a games room that is all sparklingly clean and neat. It has a marvellous atmosphere simply because it is so unspoilt.

The pub serves an incredible range of good, hand-pumped beer, including guest beers that change regularly. The food menu is wide-ranging and written up on large blackboards. Vegetarian meals and children's meals are also available.

There is a patio outside with picnic tables where well-behaved dogs are permitted.

Opening hours are 12 noon to 2 pm and 5 pm to 11 pm Monday to Thursday; 12 noon to 11 pm on Friday and Saturday; and 12 noon to 10.30 pm Sunday.

✆ 01778 342219.

How to get there: Deeping St James lies between Spalding and Stamford. Turn off the A16(T), ½ mile east of Market Deeping and follow the B1525 to the B1166, then turn left into the village.

Parking: There is ample parking at the side of the pub, with an overflow car park adjacent.

Length of the walk: 2½ miles. Map: OS Landranger 142 Peterborough (GR 153094).

THE WALK

1 From the pub car park, walk toward the side entrance of the pub, then turn right and follow the small path through the outdoor seating area, keeping the boundary hedge on your left. Go through the gap and turn left along the path.

2 Upon reaching the road (Hereward Way), cross over, turn left and then turn right towards Bell Bridge. Continue straight forward past the bridge until you reach the Crown and Anchor pub and then cross the River Welland by the narrow bridge on High Lock.

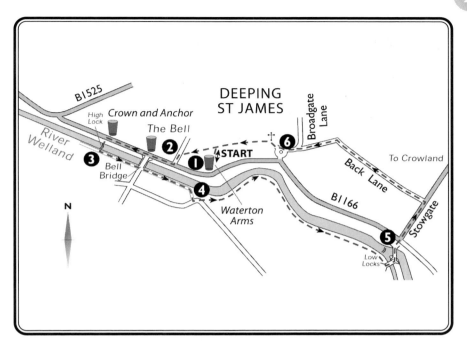

3 Turn left along the attractive embankment lane, with the river now on your left. Cross the road by the side of Bell Bridge (1651) to continue along by the river and ahead along Riverside (lane).

4 At the road junction bear left for a few yards and at the bend in the road, turn left onto a signposted path with two handgates and a fieldgate.

The church dominates much of the walk and its size reflects its origins as a church connected to a monastic foundation. In this flat area it is said that it can be seen from 10 miles away.

Continue along this attractive path, following the bends in the river for almost a mile until you reach the Low Locks.

Cross the river here, then walk left to cross the bridge over the weir and on to Eastgate.

5 Go straight across the road and walk up Stowgate for about 200 yards. Turn left along Back Lane, with its intriguing narrow strips of gardens, and round the left-hand bend in the road towards the church.

6 At Churchgate, walk straight forward, leaving the village green triangle on your left and then turn right into the churchyard. At the entrance to the church, bear very slightly left, with the hall wall on your immediate left and the enormous cemetery on your right. At the path junction continue straight forward along the same path (don't turn right) until you reach the path on your left leading back into the pub car park.

The Castle Inn

THIS ROUTE, WHICH CAN BE SHORTENED IF YOU WISH, IS A PLEASANT, UNDEMANDING CIRCUIT, TAKING IN THE CASTLE EARTHWORKS AND EVEN THE REMAINS OF MEDIEVAL FISHPONDS.

Castle Bytham is certainly one of the most interesting and scenic stone-built villages in the county. It is situated in a bowl and has all the attractions of a hillside village, plus a little stream flowing down to the River Glen. The huge, grassy earthworks are all that now remain of the once formidable castle. It was probably strengthened shortly after the Norman Conquest in 1066 by William the Conqueror's brother-in-law, Drogo. The Saxon owner before the Conquest was Earl Morcar, whose name lives on in Morkery Wood to the west of the village.

THE CASTLE INN is several hundred years old and is reputed to possess a sealed passage leading to the mound where the castle motte and bailey formerly stood. A freehouse, the Castle offers well-kept handpumped local real ales, and there is always a guest beer available. An excellent selection of home-cooked food is served in the open-plan, stone-built lounge bar, which has interesting inglenooks and, in season, a welcoming open fire. There is also a cosy restaurant where the beauty of this historic building, which has been lovingly restored, can be enjoyed.

Opening hours are 12 noon to 3 pm and 5.30 pm to 11 pm, Tuesday to Friday; 12 noon to 11 pm on Saturday and Sunday. The inn is closed all day Monday.

✆ 01780 410504.

How to get there: Turn off the A1 on the Stamford to Grantham section, onto the Castle Bytham signposted road, 10 miles north of Stamford or 3 miles south of the Colsterworth roundabout. Castle Bytham is 3½ miles off the main road, along the winding lane past Morkery Wood.
Parking: The inn does not have a car park but there is some limited roadside parking outside the pub and in the immediate vicinity.
Length of the walk: 2¼ miles or 1 mile. Map: OS Landranger 130 Grantham and surrounding area (GR 990184)

THE WALK

1. Turn up the signposted passage at the side of the Castle Inn, leading up to the church, and continue along the passage, with the stone wall on your right. At the end of the wall turn right up the tarmac path, with a wooden fence on your left, and walk on into the small estate.

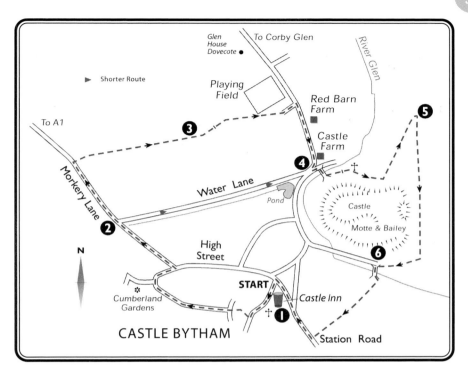

Walk forward through Cumberland Gardens to turn right down to Morkery Lane. At the lane, turn left downhill. If you wish, you may shorten the walk by turning right down Water Lane, to rejoin the route near Castle Farm (Point 4).

2 Otherwise, climb for about 260 yards from Water Lane and there turn right off the road onto a signposted path. There are two public rights of way from this spot, but proceed diagonally right across the field for 470 yards, aiming for the prominent gable end of the house.

3 At the garden corner, cross the stile and turn left, with a fence on your right, over the small paddock for 50 yards. Cross the next stile and follow the winding grass path (with a fence to your right) for 95 yards to the playing field, passing two mounds on your left. Bear right across the playing field to the far right-hand corner just beyond the swings. Here, turn right through the wooden gate for 25 yards, then left to the road. Cross the road, turn right and then proceed down the road for about 220 yards. At the end of the high wall of Castle Farm, cross the track to the signpost and footbridge over the stream. Go straight across the road here if you have walked down Water Lane.

4 Turn left after crossing the bridge, with the castle mound over on your right. Go over the paddock to a stile and then walk forward for 40 yards to the first of a series of short waymarked posts. Here, bear right uphill, following the posts and, at the fourth one, bear left on a ridge to the final post near the top corner of the field. Proceed to the stile and footbridge in the hedge.

5 Cross the footbridge to turn right, downhill, with the hedge on your right. Go over two more stiles and, upon reaching the cricket pitch set in a bowl by the river, turn right after the stile, at the side of a metal fieldgate and pavilion. Cross the next stile by the gate and go ahead for 80 yards.

6 It would be possible to proceed straight back into the village from this point. Otherwise, turn left over the substantial metal footbridge across the infant River Glen. Then, turn left for a few yards, then right and, with a hedge on your right, proceed uphill. The curious hollows on the right are the remains of medieval fishponds. In the field corner near the hilltop, cross the stile and continue ahead on the narrow path alongside the house to Station Road. The house on the left here was once the New Inn. Turn right, downhill, along Station Road into the High Street to return to the pub.

4 PINCHBECK

The Ship

A WALK FROM AN EXTRAORDINARY BACKWATER TOWARDS SURFLEET'S CURIOUSLY TILTED CHURCH TOWER AND SPIRE, ALONG THE LITTLE RIVER GLEN, NEAR THE END OF ITS 30-MILE JOURNEY TO JOIN THE WELLAND, AND BY FIELD UPON FIELD OF VEGETABLES OF ALL KINDS.

●◆●

Pinchbeck is a well-populated village and was a place of some importance in Saxon times, when it was attached to Crowland Abbey. Prosperity in the past came from flax and hemp but, nowadays, the parish covers thousands of acres of rich fenland, growing many different kinds of vegetables. At one time, there were around 100 employees at the flax mill by the river bridge.

THE SHIP is a picturesque, thatched, 400-year-old inn, in a riverside location. It has a comfortable open-plan lounge bar, with attractive alcoves around the neat central bar servery, and is especially notable for its friendly, relaxed atmosphere. There is a large garden and a play area for children.

Apart from a good selection of sandwiches, the extensive bar menu may include starters such as home-smoked duck breast with raspberry dressing, the Ship's special smokies, and Oriental chicken salad. For the main course, there are dishes such as freshly grilled mullet, the Ship's mixed grill, sea trout, or the Ship's special chicken – a chicken breast wrapped in smoked bacon and stuffed with garlic butter prawns. In addition there is a blackboard menu indicating the speciality of the day and a Thai menu from which orders have to be made at least 24 hours in advance. This is a Courage house and the beers are Best Bitter, John Smith's Bitter, and Chestnut Mild.

Opening hours are 12 noon to 2.30 pm and 7 pm to 11 pm Monday to Friday; 12 noon to 4.30 pm and 6.30 pm to 11 pm on Saturday; and 12 noon to 3 pm and 7 pm to 10.30 pm on Sunday.

☎ 01775 723792.

How to get there: Turn off the Boston to Stamford road (the A16), 2½ miles north of Spalding, onto the B1180 Bourne road. The Ship Inn is below the embankment on the right as you drive over the railway bridge, near the water tower.

Parking: There is ample parking at the Ship but if you are leaving a car while you are doing the walk, please park away from the main entrance.

Length of the walk: 4 miles but the route can be reduced by turning back at the first bridge and walking along the river path. Map: OS Landranger 131 Boston and surrounding area (GR 235260).

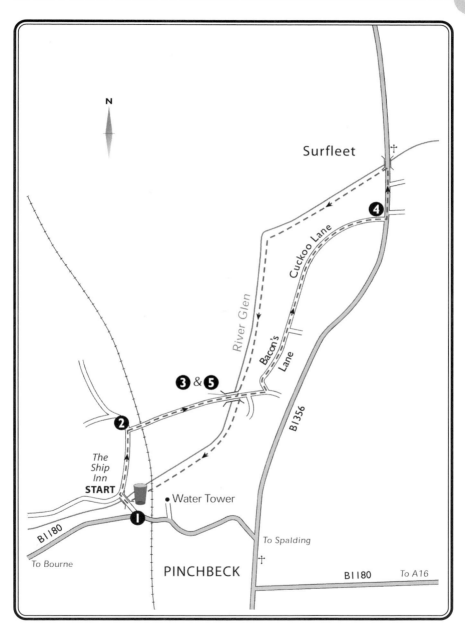

N

Surfleet

Cuckoo Lane

River Glen

Bacon's Lane

❸ & ❺

❷

❹

B1356

The
Ship
Inn
START

• Water Tower

❶

B1180

To Spalding

To Bourne

PINCHBECK

B1180   To A16

THE WALK

1 From the inn car park, turn right and walk up Northgate, over the river and almost immediately right up Herring Lane, with an unusual house on your right.

2 After about 500 yards, turn right up Langhole Drove to the railway crossing. Go over the crossing and walk forward for some 450 yards and over the river bridge.

3 *For the shorter walk:* Turn right to walk along the riverside path. Continue the walk at point 5.

For the longer walk: Continue round to the left, then left up Bacon's Lane. Go left at the junction, Cuckoo Lane, walking towards the leaning tower and spire of the church at Surfleet along the narrow lane.

4 Turn left at the main road for 250 yards and, at the beginning of the footway for the road bridge, turn left over the stile, with the River Glen on your right. The footpath is signposted here 'Pinchbeck Station, 1¾ miles'. Follow this riverside path until you meet the bridge over the Glen once again. Cross the lane and continue ahead with the river still on your right.

5 Continue along the riverside path until you reach the water tower and a stile in order to cross the railway. Then go over another stile and the path leads you directly into the car park of the Ship inn.

The Rising Sun

THIS IS A WALK WITH A DIFFERENCE, ALONG SEA BANKS, OLD AND NEW, WITH EXCELLENT BIRD-WATCHING OPPORTUNITIES, ESPECIALLY DURING THE WINTER MONTHS.

The salt marshes in this area of Lincolnshire have a unique flora because of the highly saline conditions and, where reclaimed, have become top quality arable land. Being set right on the edge of the east coast, you may see a beautiful sunrise across the marshes.

THE RISING SUN offers a warm and friendly welcome to a wide variety of customers, including members of the farming community, aircraft enthusiasts observing the spectacular

NATO aircraft during their training on the adjacent bombing range, wildfowlers and bird-watchers, and, of course, walkers. This one-room pub was built in 1723 and the attractive lounge bar has bench seating, with an open fire whenever the weather merits one. Outside is a secluded beer garden and there is a play area for children.

Real ale is served, as well as fresh bar snacks, and a range of good-value dishes, such as rump steak and home-cooked ham.

Opening hours are 12 noon to 3 pm (to 4 pm on Saturday) and 7 pm to 11 pm (to 10.30 pm on Sunday).

☎ 01406 550474.

How to get there: Turn off the A17(T) King's Lynn to Sleaford road at Gedney onto the B1359. Gedney Drove End is 5½ miles along this road, via Gedney Dyke.

Parking: Customers may leave their cars in the pub car park, with the permission of the landlord, while they do the walk. Alternatively, roadside parking may be available in the village or you could park in the small car park on the seaward side of White House Farm at point 4 and stop for refreshment halfway through your walk.

Length of the walk: 3¼ miles. Map: OS Landranger 131 Boston and surrounding area (GR 463293).

THE WALK

1 Turn left out of the car park for 300 yards along the road and then turn right on the signposted footpath for 200 or so yards to a bridge and an old sea bank. Cross the bridge and turn right along the bank until you reach the lane.

2 Turn left up the lane past the farm buildings and, on reaching the T-junction, walk straight forward on the signposted path to the sea. You should keep off the salt

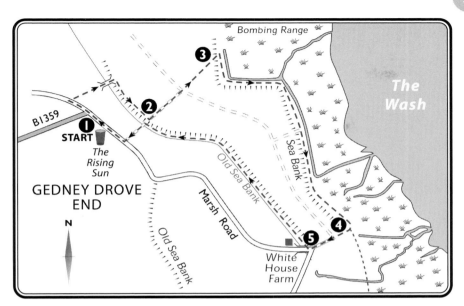

marshes themselves. The area can be dangerous without local knowledge as you may find yourself cut off when the tide comes in quickly. The creeks are deep and they are sometimes hidden.

3 Climb the sea bank and turn right to follow it round the various bends until you reach the bank-top triple-armed signpost, with the metal fieldgate and wooden handgate leading down to the track and the metalled lane.

4 Follow these down to your right off the embankment towards White House Farm.

5 Leave the lane to turn right along the Old Sea Bank just before the main road and continue, with the dyke on your left, until you reach your original lane. Turn left down the lane and right at the main road, back into the village and your starting place.

The Welby Arms

A MOST PLEASANT WALK BY A TRANQUIL DISUSED CANAL AND ALONG THE BANK OF AN ATTRACTIVE RESERVOIR.

The ancient village of Denton is recorded in the Domesday Book as Dentune, meaning 'village in a valley'. It was once part of the Forest of Kesteven and trees still dominate part of the landscape. In the middle of the 17th century the manor of Denton was sold to William Welby, MP, and the village pub is now owned by the Welby Estate.

THE WELBY ARMS dates back to 1662, but much of the pub and village history was lost in 1917, when records perished in a fire that destroyed Denton Manor. Strange, then, that in the pub is an old picture of nearby Stoke Rochford Hall, which itself was recently gutted by fire.

There is an attractive beer garden at the front of the pub and, inside, an interesting horseshoe-shaped bar area, with two cosy fires. There are beams and old pictures and a separate restaurant for 25 diners.

The friendly landlords offer an extensive menu including steaks, chicken, duck, fish dishes, pies and vegetarian options as well as a traditional Sunday lunch. There is a good choice of beers, and chilled wine is available by the glass.

Meals are served Monday to Saturday from 12 noon to 2 pm and from 7 pm to 9.30 pm, and on Sunday from 12 noon to 2 pm only.

☎ 01476 870304.

How to get there: Turn off the A1 south-west of Grantham onto the A607 Melton Mowbray road and continue for 2 miles before turning right into Denton.
Parking: The pub car park.
Length of the walk: 2¾ or 3¼ miles. Map: OS Landranger 130 Grantham and surrounding area (GR 865325).

THE WALK

1 Turn left out of the pub car park. At the junction, with the pub on your right, turn left down Church Street. At the next junction with Belvoir Road, continue ahead to the right-hand bend, with a lane to the left.

2 Turn right at the bend and 300 yards beyond it, turn left on the signposted path, just past the undertakers and before Briery House.

3 Climb the stile and walk towards the spire of Harlaxton church in the distance. On descending into the valley, you will find a bridge, with handrails, over the stream. Cross the bridge and continue ahead up the rise to a stile and gate.

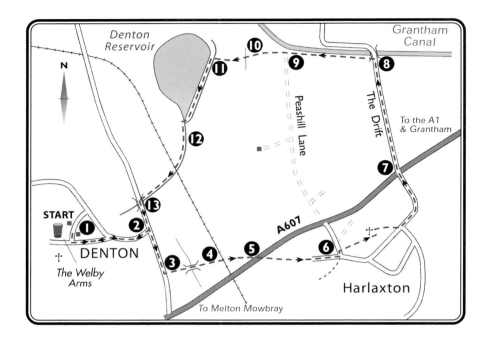

④ Turn right on the old railway and shortly turn left over another stile. Walk diagonally right up the field on the defined path to the main road, aiming for the furthest of the large trees on the right and a stile in the top right-hand corner of the field.

⑤ Cross the road and proceed diagonally left on the signposted path toward the two gable ends, where, in the corner by the stone wall, you will find a stile leading into a small lane called West End.

⑥ *For the shorter route:* Turn left to cross the main road and continue ahead down Peashill Lane to rejoin the route at point 9.

For the longer route: Take the signposted footpath through the kissing gates leading you to the church. Walk on past the front of the church to the far side, turn left, then take the metalled path leading to the right and not the path proceeding straight to a cottage. At the end of your path, go down the stone steps into Church Street and turn left along High Street to the crossroads, with a number of interesting houses to be seen en route.

7 Cross the main road and continue ahead down The Drift.

8 After 900 yards and just before reaching Harlaxton Bridge over the canal, turn left up the steps to the stile on the signposted footpath and walk across the grass field, with the canal on your right. Continue alongside the canal, crossing two further stiles, until you reach another stile alongside a metal fieldgate where the canal turns right.

9 Go over the stile ahead and bear left across the paddock with the hedge on your left, until you reach the footbridge, with a stile in the far left-hand field corner.

10 Cross the bridge and continue ahead over two further fields, keeping the hedge on your left.

11 After crossing the next bridge, climb the steps to the bank of Denton reservoir and turn left. Follow this wide track and continue forward over the bridge ahead immediately after the first bridge on the right.

12 Cross the second footbridge on the right and then turn left, with the stream now on your left. Climb the stile and cross the line of the old mineral railway and continue forward over more stiles to the lane.

13 At the lane, turn left into Denton village and, at the junction, turn right to retrace your steps back to the pub.

The Tally Ho Inn

THIS IS AN UNDEMANDING WALK THAT EXPLORES LEVEL FOOTPATHS, BRIDLEWAYS AND LANES. THERE IS ONLY ONE MODERATE HILL, YET THE ROUTE OFFERS ATTRACTIVE, UNEXPECTED VIEWS OVER WOODED COUNTRYSIDE, ENORMOUS FIELDS AND DISTANT VILLAGES, WITH INTRIGUING NAMES LIKE SCOTT WILLOUGHBY. INDEED, SOME SECTIONS OF THE WALK SEEM SURPRISINGLY REMOTE DESPITE THE PROXIMITY OF AN 'A' ROAD.

***

Many years ago, the village of Aswarby was removed by order of the squire whilst the great house at Aswarby which was long home to the Whichcotes family, was destroyed by a disastrous fire and pulled down in 1947. The church and a few grey stone cottages remain at the entrance to the hall grounds.

THE TALLY HO INN is situated away from the village among gently, rolling wooded countryside on a bend in the road. This welcoming 17th-century building has been a hostelry and coach stop on the Bourne to Sleaford road for over 100 years. Its stables and dairy are now converted into six very pleasant en suite bedrooms and in the pub itself there are lots of old beams, comfortable seating and a stone fireplace, with log fires in winter, making the lounge bar snug and cosy. Hunting pictures adorn the walls.

The pub is justifiably proud of its reputation for good wholesome traditional food which ranges from Sunday roasts through to light bar snacks such as toasted sandwiches and baguettes. The beers include Batemans XB and XXXB and Everards Tiger.

Opening hours are 12 noon to 2.30 pm and 6 pm to 11 pm Monday to Saturday; and 12 noon to 2.30 pm and 7 pm to 10.30 pm on Sunday.
✆ 01529 455205.

How to get there: The inn is situated on the A15 Sleaford to Bourne road some 4 miles south of the Sleaford bypass roundabout and 13 miles north of Bourne.
Parking: There is some parking in front of the inn, with additional parking behind. It is only courteous, though, to inform the landlord if you intend to leave your car there whilst you walk and then to park away from the front door.
Length of the walk: 4½ miles. Map: OS Landranger 130 Grantham and surrounding area (GR 061395).

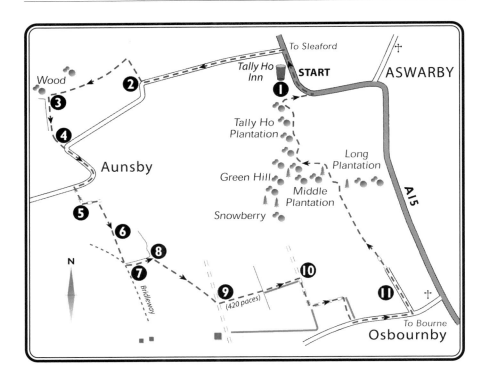

THE WALK

1 From the inn, turn left along the main road towards Sleaford for 200 yards and then left again up the quiet lane leading to Aunsby.

2 At the first left-hand bend in the road, turn right on a waymarked signposted bridleway. Turn left at the first hedge, with the hedge and ditch on your immediate left.

3 Halfway along the wood on the right, turn left over the bridge across the ditch and proceed forward with a ditch on your right until you reach the lane leading into Aunsby.

4 At the lane, walk straight forward into the village and just round the bend by the council houses, opposite Ash Cottage, turn left to follow the grass track on the signposted diverted bridleway.

5 Bear left for 100 yards on the track and go through the metal fieldgate to turn right uphill, along the line of trees on your right.

6 Continue forward past the electricity pylon and down the slope to the bridleway bridge.

7 After crossing the bridge, turn left on the footpath along the edge of the dyke on the left for 400 yards to the dyke corner.

8 Then bear diagonally right across the field to a point on the track leading up from the abandoned farm buildings. Aim for a point about midway between the distant church spire and the farm buildings.

9 Cross the farm track (waymark) and go forward over the field to proceed towards another ditch corner. Continue forward with the ditch on your left and cross the bridge in the corner of the field.

10 Turn right on the grass track and near the field corner turn left for 70 yards. Go through the metal gate and turn right alongside the bushes to the next metal gate by the road and turn left along the road.

11 Upon reaching Osbournby's extraordinarily wide village square, turn left up North Street. At the end of the metalled lane, continue uphill along the wide grass track with the hedge on your left. There is a seat at the top of the hill for you to rest and enjoy the view. Cross the brow of the hill with Long Plantation on your right, then go downhill along the left edge of the large field, skirting Middle Plantation and Tally Ho Plantation. On reaching the stream (waymark) turn right with the stream on your left until you reach the little copse and bridge and a signpost on the main road. Turn left round the bend in the road to the Tally Ho Inn, exercising proper caution on the busy road.

The Malcolm Arms

THIS IS A WATERSIDE WALK, WITH A RIVER, WIDE DRAINS AND LAKES, ALL SUPPORTING PLENTY OF BIRD LIFE AND THERE IS A GOOD CHANCE OF SEEING DEER IN THE SMALL NATURE RESERVE OPPOSITE THE MALCOLM ARMS.

The word 'gowt' means a sluice but the more common name locally is Anton's Gowt Lock. At various points on this route, you will catch glimpses of the magnificent lantern tower of St Botolph's church in Boston which rises to 272½ ft. It was completed in 1460, although the foundations were begun in 1309, and it has been a guide to travellers by land and sea for centuries. You can decide for yourself whether it merits the local name of the Boston Stump.

THE MALCOLM ARMS is a fine Victorian inn which has been considerably extended and tastefully modernised. There is a splendid conservatory dining room that is a lovely light place to eat, overlooking the garden. There is also an outside patio area, a family room and a games room. In summertime, the pub is a haunt for both anglers and boating enthusiasts from the nearby River Witham.

The food is listed on an incredible 46-selection bar meal menu, including a large range of cold meat and fish salads, whilst the restaurant menu offers 52 different dishes. The Sunday lunch is outstanding value, and there is a good selection of vegetarian meals and a separate children's menu. Well-kept Bateman and Tetley Pedigree beers are on handpump and draught Guinness and a good selection of lagers and ciders are also available.

Opening hours are 12 noon to 2.30 pm and 7 pm to 11 pm Monday to Thursday; 11.30 am to 11 pm Friday; 11 am to 11 pm Saturday; and 12 noon to 11 pm on Sunday. Food is not served at all on Monday nor on Tuesday lunchtime but is available the rest of the time.

How to get there: Turn north off the A1121 Swineshead Bridge to Boston road at Hubbert's Bridge onto the B1192. Continue to Langrick where Anton's Gowt is signposted. Alternatively, from the B1183 Boston to Horncastle road, turn off to Anton's Gowt at Cowbridge.

Parking: Customers may leave their cars in the pub car park while they are doing the walk but do please park away from the main entrance. There is also limited off-road parking by the road bridge at the side of the lock gates.

Length of the walk: 3 miles or a short option of ¾ mile. Map: OS Landranger 131 Boston and surrounding area (GR 301475)

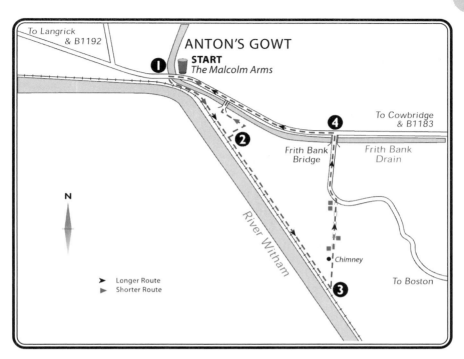

THE WALK

1 Turn right out of the car park for a few yards to the road bridge on the bend and then go left on the signposted path, with the lock gates on your left. Cross the line of the old railway to turn left over the bridge, with the broad River Witham on your right and the lock-keeper's cottage and his extensive garden on the left. Walk forward along the river bank for about 350 yards, with the abandoned railway beside you and Boston Stump directly ahead.

2 *For the shorter walk:* At the end of the iron fence and the footpath sign, turn left off the riverside path. Cross the line of the old railway and follow the waymarked path round the line of the newly extended nature reserve. This public footpath has been diverted and the new route may not be shown on OS maps. It is a good wide path with trees on the left and a fence on the right. At the end of the deer paddock, turn left alongside Frith Drain and continue as far as the large wooden bridge. Cross the bridge and turn left up the road, with the modern Holland House on your right and the lakes of the nature reserve across the drain on your left. Deer may often be seen sheltering in the trees by the lakes. The Malcolm Arms is just up the road.

For the longer walk: Continue along the river bank for another mile and turn left off it at the three-fingered metal signpost situated after the industrial chimney, going between the old metal gate and the wooden one.

3 The public footpath actually goes through the building complex of the old station yard and by the foot of the chimney, but generations of local people have avoided doing so by walking down the far better track on the opposite side of the hedge, that is, keeping the hedgeline and ditch on your immediate left until you reach the lane, where, in fact, the path is signposted showing this route. Walk up to the lane junction and turn left opposite a thatched house and around the road bends for ½ mile until you reach the bridge over the Frith Drain.

4 Go over this bridge and turn left back to the Malcolm Arms.

The Bell Inn

THE WALK TAKES IN ONE OF THE MOST ATTRACTIVE PARTS OF THE VIKING WAY LONG-DISTANCE RECREATIONAL PATH, WHERE THIS SECTION ALONG THE NARROW WESTERN RIDGE, CALLED 'THE CLIFF' JOINS A STRING OF STONE-BUILT, SPRING-LEAF VILLAGES, WITH EXTENSIVE VIEWS OVER THE WITHAM VALLEY AND ONWARDS TO THE RIVER TRENT AND NOTTINGHAMSHIRE.

—●●—

The delightful village of Coleby, some seven miles south of Lincoln, has an interesting mix of old buildings. The medieval church of All Saints has a crocketed spire which was added in the 15th century and the village pub, the Bell, is said to derive its name from the fact that the five bells in the church tower were cast in specially-prepared holes in a nearby field. That field is now the pub car park. It is also recorded that the first landlord of the pub was called Thomas Bell.

THE BELL, situated in Far Lane directly behind the church, offers a contemporary dining experience whilst still retaining the history and character of a pub dating back to 1759. The low-beamed ceilings and roaring log fires during the colder months make for an especially warm welcome. There is a large restaurant and an attractive terrace, with decking and heaters, and the pub also has rooms to hire for private functions.

The food menu has dishes to tempt everyone, from steaks, chicken, pork, and fish through to pasta and vegetarian options. There is an excellent choice of drink, with three hand-pulled ales always available and a comprehensive wine list. Visit the pub's own website: www.thebellinncoleby.co.uk for sample menus.

Opening hours are 11.30 am to 3.30 pm and 5.30 pm to 11 pm Monday to Saturday; and 12 noon to 10.30 pm on Sunday.

✆ 01522 810240.

How to get there: Coleby is signposted off the A607 Lincoln to Grantham road between Harmston and Boothby Graffoe.

Parking: Customers may park in the pub car park while they are doing the walk. Alternatively, there is roadside parking at the side of the village green at the bottom of High Street.

Length of the walk: 2½ miles. Map: OS Landranger 121 Lincoln and surrounding area (GR 976607).

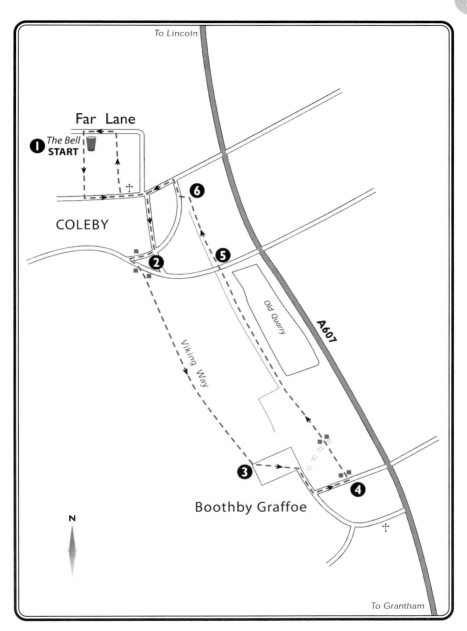

THE WALK

1. Turn left out of the car park to the end of Far Lane and go through the kissing gate on the left of the metal fieldgate. Turn left, then left off the path after only a few yards, at the gate leading you into Church Lane. Walk up the lane, with the church on your left, and turn right at the road junction to walk down High Street. At the bottom, walk across the triangle of the village green, with the Tempest Arms pub on your right.

2. Turn left up the narrow, signposted path with a Viking Way waymark, with No 3 Hill Rise on your right, and continue on this well-marked path along the cliff edge for about ¾ mile until you near Boothy Graffoe.

3. Turn left (waymark) through the kissing gate by the metal fieldgate on your left and walk diagonally across the grass paddock to the gates in the far right-hand corner of the field. Walk down Far End Lane, with Keeper's Cottage, and often a painted gypsy caravan, on the right. At the road junction with Main Street, turn left, uphill, with the attractive little green public enclosure called Henson's Lawn on your right. It is a good place for an apple stop.

4. After about 150 yards, turn left up four concrete steps onto a signposted footpath, with a stile, and continue along the narrow pathway until the end of the garden, to a gate and stile. Cross the small paddock to a step stile, with the fence on your immediate right. Go over the farm track to walk between two farm buildings (waymark), then through the metal fieldgate to go straight forward across the arable field, walking directly towards Coleby church spire. At the hedge corner you will meet a track. Continue along this until you meet the lane leading into Coleby.

5 Cross this lane and continue straight forward, with the stone wall on your left.

6 At the wooden fence to your front, turn left down the alleyway (this path has been diverted and may not be as shown on the OS map) and on into Blind Lane. Turn right, with the school on your left, and then left towards the church. Walk up Church Lane to turn right up the path leading to the church, which is well worth a visit, and follow this round through the graveyard, on to Far Lane and your starting place.

The Lord Nelson

T HE VILLAGE OF DUNHOLME, SAVED NOWADAYS BY A BYPASS,
IS A QUIET BACKWATER, WITH AN OLD CHURCH AND
CHURCHYARD SHADED BY BEECH AND CHESTNUT TREES. IT IS
SITED NEAR THE CLEAR WATERS OF THE BECK FLOWING DOWN TO
JOIN THE INFANT LANGWORTH RIVER. THE WALK TAKES YOU
THROUGH A NATURE RESERVE, THE GIFT OF A LOCAL
INHABITANT, AND ALONG THE ANCIENT ASHING LANE, ONCE A
CART ROUTE ACROSS THE FORD TO A LONG FORGOTTEN RAILWAY
HALT.

THE LORD NELSON is a friendly village local whose comfortable lounge bar is dedicated to No 170 Squadron of the RAF which was stationed at nearby Dunholme Lodge during the Second World War. There is a separate bar and games room, with a beer garden outside.

It is open on Monday to Friday from 2 pm to 11 pm (usually from 12 noon during the summer); 12 noon to 11 pm Saturday; and 12 noon to 10.30 pm on Sunday.

☎ 01673 860101.

How to get there: The Lord Nelson is situated on the old main road off the Dunholme bypass (the A46 Lincoln to Grimsby road), 10 miles south-west of Market Rasen and 6 miles north-east of Lincoln.

Parking: Patrons may leave their cars in the large pub car park whilst they are doing the walk. Alternatively, there is limited roadside parking available by the war memorial, opposite the church.

Length of the walk: 3½ miles or 1½ miles. Map: OS Landranger 121 or Explorer 272 (GR 026790).

THE WALK

1 Turn left out of the pub car park and walk along the road.

2 Turn left over a footbridge across the beck by the entrance to the church and left again to follow the tarmac path along the beckside. At the ford turn right for about 80 yards, then left at the T-junction and on to the signposted public footpath. Walk forward through the handgate and continue, with the fence on your right, to the next gate.

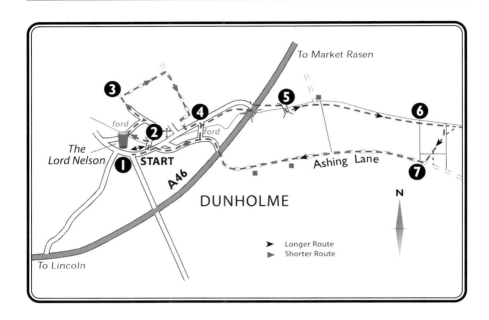

3 Go through the gate and turn right to walk along the wide track over the field and go right again at the path junction on a signposted bridleway. On meeting the road again, turn left for about 170 yards to Beck Lane.

4 *For the shorter walk:* Cross the footbridge at the side of the ford and, at the lane junction, turn right to follow the lane back to the start.

For the longer walk: Do not go down Beck Lane, but continue forward a few yards to the Anglian Water pumping station. Follow the signposted footpath, with the hedge on your immediate left. Continue on the grassy footpath to the signpost and footbridge at the far right-hand corner of the field. Cross the bypass road to the steps by the road sign to Dunholme and go diagonally left for 100 yards to the footbridge.

5 Cross the bridge and turn left, with the beck on your left, for about 1,000 yards until you reach Pickering Meadow Nature Reserve.

6 Walk forward and turn right, just beyond the seats, to a handgate, then follow the mown path across the meadow to a gap between the hedges and an earth bridge. Cross the next paddock to a wooden field gate, with a stile on the right, to turn right along Ashing Lane.

7 Follow the lane along for about ¾ mile until you reach the main road. Proceed directly across the road and go down the embankment slope, with its non-slip bricks, to follow Ashing Lane, signposted as a bridleway. Continue past the new churchyard and the war memorial to rejoin your earlier route and return to the Lord Nelson car park.

The Marmion Arms

THE CLOSING DECADES OF THE 18TH CENTURY SAW CANAL
CONSTRUCTION IN MANY PARTS OF ENGLAND. IN 1786 THE
TATTERSHALL CANAL WAS OPENED, LINKING TATTERSHALL TO
THE RIVER WITHAM AND LATER, TO HORNCASTLE BY
CANALIZING THE RIVER BAIN. TODAY THE CANAL IS DISUSED
BUT MAKES A PLEASANT COMPANION TO THIS GENTLE STROLL,
TAKING IN THE VILLAGES OF KIRKBY ON BAIN AND HALTHAM.

THE MARMION ARMS takes its name from the ancient family of the King's Champions, an honour bestowed upon Sir Robert Marmion by William the Conqueror in 1086. The present Queen's Champion, Colonel Sir John Dymoke resides in an estate close by. The pub is believed to be the only timber-framed, wattle and daub, thatched property of its kind in Lincolnshire and, possibly, in the country. It has a spacious bar, a separate dining room and a pleasant beer garden.

This friendly hostelry offers traditional home-made fare, including sirloin steak, steak and ale pie, gammon and lasagne. Lighter options such as jacket potatoes, burger and chips and sausage and chips are also available. John Smith's, Fosters, Kronenberg, Budweiser, Guinness and Strongbow cider are some of the drinks served.

The opening times are 12 noon to 2 pm and 7 pm to 11 pm Monday to Saturday; 12 noon to 10.30 pm on Sunday.
✆ 01507 568326.

How to get there: Haltham is on the A153 Sleaford road, 5 miles south of Horncastle.
Parking: In the large car park opposite the pub.
Length of the walk: 2¾ miles. Map: OS Landranger 122 Skegness and surrounding area (GR 247637).

THE WALK

1 From the pub car park, walk ahead past the side of the pub down West Lane.

2 After 330 yards, immediately after a bungalow called Fieldview, turn left up a short cul-de-sac. Pass to the right of The Cottages and go over a stile straight ahead. With the stream just down to your right, follow the faint path ahead

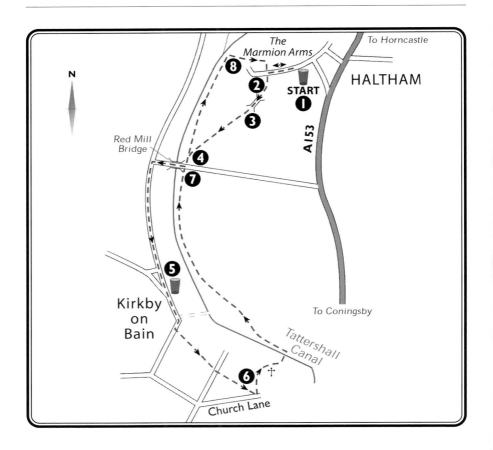

over the field, aiming for the prominent curve in the bushes. At the far end of the bushes, bear right for 50 yards to some waymarks and an earth bridge over the stream.

3 Cross diagonally left over the next large field to Red Mill Bridge in the far corner.

4 Climb the stile and turn right over the bridge to a road junction and then turn left down the road to Kirkby on Bain.

5　Continue ahead past the Ebrington Arms pub on the left and, at the sharp right-hand bend in the road, continue round for approximately 70 yards, passing Bain House on your right. Then, at the next house, turn left across the road to a small metal safety barrier and the wooden kissing gate behind it. Go through the gate and continue on the signposted footpath. At the next road, with another small metal safety barrier, turn left for 10 yards, then right to cross the road. Go ahead through a gate onto a metalled path, passing the school, and ahead through another gate.

6　On meeting Church Lane, with its oval grass roundabout, turn left and go through a handgate in the churchyard, passing the church on your right. Bear slightly right to cross a long concrete bridge with white handrails. Turn immediately left over the stile to walk alongside the canal. Pass over another stile, then about 40 yards from an old wooden bridge, bear right at a waymark, then left skirting conifers on your left. Cross the next stile and continue ahead to the canal bank, passing the old canal blocks and a house on your left. Follow the bank ahead to Red Mill Bridge.

7　Cross both stiles alongside the bridge and continue ahead to Haltham lock, crossing two further stiles en route.

8　At Haltham Lock, with its bridge and four-fingered signpost, turn right across the grass field for 100 yards to a wooden bridge to the left of a bungalow. Continue ahead up the narrow grass path, then turn right on a broad grass path back to West Lane. Turn left to return to the pub.

The Blue Bell Inn

LINCOLNSHIRE CAN BE SEEN AT ITS BEST ON THIS VARIED CIRCULAR WALK, WITH THE EVER-CHANGING COLOURS OF THE FIELD PATTERNS ACROSS THE WOLD AND SOME MAGNIFICIENT VIEWS EN ROUTE. ON A CLEAR DAY, LINCOLN CATHEDRAL, SOME 20 MILES AWAY, CAN BE SPIED FROM FULLETBY TOP.

THE BLUE BELL INN, which is some 200 years old, is in the small village of Belchford, in an Area of Outstanding Natural Beauty, at the very heart of the Lincolnshire Wolds. It is situated on the Viking Way long-distance recreational path which actually passes the door where walkers are made most welcome.

Comfortably furnished, it is tastefully decorated and has two open fireplaces in the bar area and a further one in the restaurant. The landlords have gained a reputation for friendly service and excellent food and such is their fame that it is essential to book a table if you would like to dine at the weekends. All the food is cooked to order using fresh ingredients, including Lincoln Red beef. The Blue Bell is a freehouse and the beers are constantly changed.

Opening hours Tuesday to Saturday are 11.30 am to 2.30 pm and 6.30 pm to 11 pm; Sunday 12 noon to 4 pm. The inn is closed all day Monday.

✆ 01507 533602.

How to get there: Turn off the A153 Horncastle to Louth road, 2 miles north of West Ashby and 3 miles south of Scamblesby. Approaching from the Bluestone Heath road to the east, turn off down Belchford Hill.

Parking: Customers may park in the pub car park, preferably in the rear car park, furthest from the entrance. Alternatively, if it is not a Sunday, there is limited parking further along the road near the church entrance.

Length of the walk: 4½ miles. Map: OS Landranger 122 or Explorer 274 (GR 292755).

THE WALK

1 From the Blue Bell car park, turn left and almost immediately right up Dams Lane, signposted 'The Viking Way'.

2 After following the lane round the bend, turn left through a gate on a signposted path, just before the gate across the

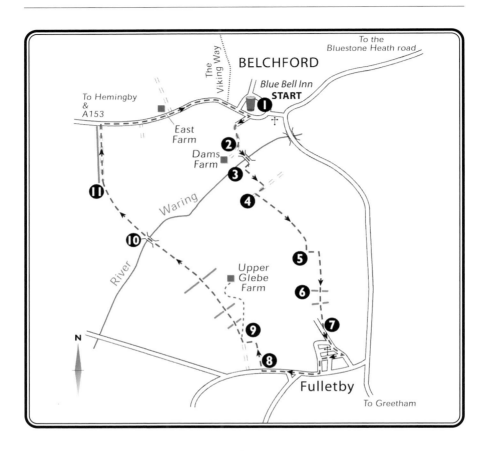

track leading to Dams Farm. Walk down to the stile, cross the footbridge and then turn right.

3 Go through the gate and turn left, with the fence on your left until the end of the field. At the stile and track, turn right and continue along the hedgeline until you meet another signpost and an opening on your left.

4 Turn left up the rise to the hedge and continue along the field edge, with the hedge on your immediate left. Follow

the hedge and walk up to the top corner of the upper field where there is a broken stile.

5   Go through the opening and turn left on a good track for 100 yards and then at the post and wooden pylon turn right, to proceed downhill with the hedge on your left.

6   At the field corner, go through the handgate and follow the hedge line on your left, down to the next gate and bridge. Then walk ahead up the rise aiming for the smaller of the two masts, with a bungalow in the foreground.

7   At the top corner of the field by the bungalow, turn left, uphill, along the lane and then right, with the church on your right. Turn left at the end of the village lane up to the main road. Turn right past the garage and keep right at the road junction.

8   Turn right down the first track on the right (not as shown on the OS map) and follow this track to the left at the gate, then round to the right, past the Old Rectory.

9   Go through the handgate by the metal fieldgate and, where the obvious track bends to the right towards the buildings of Upper Glebe Farm, continue forward, with the hedge on your left, to a gate and stile. The route of the bridleway should be clearly defined down the next three fields as it leads you down to a stout bridge across the infant River Waring.

10 After crossing the bridge, walk straight forward, uphill, on a defined right of way over the arable field that used to be Belchford Common.

11 Continue with the hedge on the left, along the good track to the road. At the road, turn right and walk down into Belchford village and back to your starting point.

The Vine Inn

THIS IS A WALK FOR NATURE LOVERS. THE STEEP SIDES AND WIDE BOTTOM OF THE SWABY VALLEY INDICATE THAT THIS WAS A GLACIAL OVERFLOW CHANNEL. THE VALLEY ITSELF IS A SITE OF SPECIAL SCIENTIFIC INTEREST FOR THE DRY, CHALKY SOIL ON THE VALLEY SIDES SUPPORTS OLD CHALK GRASSLAND, RARE TODAY IN LINCOLNSHIRE. CONTROLLED GRAZING ENCOURAGES PLANTS SUCH AS WILD THYME AND SMALL SCABIOUS WHILE THE RICH MARSH IN THE VALLEY BOTTOM IN ITS UNDRAINED STATE PROVIDES A GOOD HABITAT FOR SNIPE AND LAPWING.

THE VINE INN is a friendly and simple place, situated at the edge of a small, comparatively remote village on the very beginnings of the Lincolnshire Wolds and only 7 miles from the sea. There are records of an ale house on the site going back to 1508 though the present building appears to be 18th century, with a more recent addition.

There is a comfortable bar and an extended dining room. The pub is extremely popular with walkers and can cater for groups up to thirty in number, with advance notice. Overnight accommodation is available and a large old world garden outside. The bar is well stocked with beer from Lincolnshire's own brewery at Wainfleet – Bateman – plus a variety of guest beers. The home-made food includes bar snacks such as sandwiches, baps, jumbo sausages in French bread and ploughman's, as well as more substantial fare.

The inn is open on Monday to Saturday from 12 noon to 11 pm, (apart from Tuesday, when it is only open in the evening from 7 pm to 10.30 pm). Sunday opening is 12 noon to 3 pm and 7 pm to 10.30 pm.

✆ 01507 480273.

How to get there: Turn off the A16(T) Louth to Ulceby Cross road, 1½ miles north-west of Ulceby Cross or, coming from Louth, 3 miles after passing through Burwell. The Vine Inn is on the edge of the only through road in the village.

Parking: Patrons may leave their cars in the pub car park whilst doing the walk but do please ask where, otherwise delivery lorries may have difficulty in negotiating the turn. Alternatively, there is space for one or two cars by the church, if it is not a Sunday.

Length of the walk: 2 or 3½ miles. Map: OS Landranger 122 (GR 401769).

PUB WALKS IN LINCOLNSHIRE

THE WALK

1 Turn left out of the inn car park towards the church and right at the lane junction. There are two signposted paths beyond the church – take the right-hand one. Very shortly, by the old sycamore and near the fence corner to your right, bear left across the paddock to the stile in the fence and then walk towards the old wind pump, keeping it just on your right, with the stream and lakes below on your left. Cross the stile in the left-hand corner of the field by Belleau bridge, then turn left over the bridge.

2 *For the shorter walk:* Continue for 350 yards. At the right-hand bend in the road, turn left onto the good, signposted bridleway track towards a woodland belt. After about 700 yards along this green lane, at the path junction (waymark), turn left and leave the bridleway. Continue from the final paragraph at point 7.

For the longer walk: Turn right into the wood on the right, on the signposted footpath, with the stream on your right. Follow the waymarked path over two small bridges and, at the end of the second bridge, bear slightly left up the rise to the footpath signpost by the wood edge.

3 At the signpost, continue ahead across the arable field, aiming to the left of Belleau church, with the fence down on your right.

4 At the ladder stile near the top of the rise, continue ahead across the top of the steep little valley to the next ladder stile just beyond a large tree. Continue forward over the next field towards the church. At the third ladder stile, bear left towards the right-hand end of the church (skirting to the right of the small bushes just in front of you). At the next stile, turn left on the lane to the T-junction.

SOUTH THORESBY – *The Vine Inn*

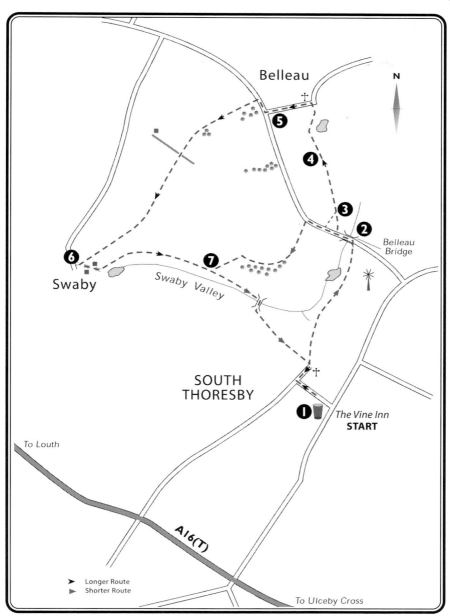

5 Turn right and by the wood turn left off the road, with the wood on your left, to cross a field, making at first for the small triangular copse. Aim for the right-hand side of the copse and then walk forward towards the field boundary hedge, just to the right of the corner. Carry on across a large field, keeping the woodland belt in the distance over on your left. In the far left-hand corner of this field, cross the stile in the fence and go down the steep little path at the edge of the wood to the stile on the lane.

6 Turn left up the lane past the houses into the Swaby valley on a good path. Continue until you meet the shorter route (waymark) joining from the left.

7 Follow the public footpath, bearing right with the stream below the bank on your right. Walk along the field edge until you come to the footbridge to your right. Cross the bridge and go over the duckboards on the far bank. Turn left at the top of the bank to walk towards South Thoresby church across this deliberately undrained marshy section. Go over the sleepers and on to the stile. Continue towards the church and go over the stile into the lane. Then retrace your steps to the car park.

The King's Head

T HE FINE NORMAN CHURCH OF ALL SAINTS, WITH ITS INTERESTING MEMORIALS AND TENNYSON CONNECTIONS, STANDS GRANDLY ABOVE THE PEACEFUL VILLAGE THROUGH WHICH THE INFANT RIVER RASE FLOWS DOWN FROM BULLY HILL. INDEED, THE COLOURFUL LANE LEADING DOWN TO THE FORD BY THE VILLAGE HALL MUST BE AS PICTURESQUE AS ANY VILLAGE STREET IN ENGLAND. THERE ARE EXHILARATING VIEWS, WITH LINCOLN CATHEDRAL IN THE DISTANCE, AND SOME QUITE STEEP SECTIONS THAT BELIE THE WIDELY-HELD BELIEF THAT LINCOLNSHIIRE IS FLAT. THE WALK IS IN AN AREA OF OUTSTANDING NATURAL BEAUTY (AONB) ON THE VERY EDGE OF THE WOLDS, PARTLY ALONG ONE OF THE BEST SECTIONS OF THE VIKING WAY LONG-DISTANCE RECREATIONAL PATH AND THROUGH A COUNTRYSIDE COMMISSION STEWARDSHIP SITE, WITH UNLIMITED PUBLIC ACCESS.

The 14th-century **KING'S HEAD** makes a very pretty picture, with its rare thatched roof and charming surroundings in a village considered by many to be the most beautiful in the Wolds. It extends a warm welcome to walkers and the extensive menu has something for everyone. The pub prides itself on its home-cooked food, made from fresh local produce, including the famous Tealby sausages. Vegetarian dishes are also available, together with a range of freshly baked baguettes.

Food is served from 12 noon to 2 pm and 6.30 pm to 9 pm on Monday to Saturday, and from 12 noon to 3 pm and 5.30 pm to 8.30 pm on Sunday.
☎ 01673 838347.

How to get there: Tealby lies 4 miles from Market Rasen on the B1203 Grimsby road. If approaching on the B1225 (known as Caistor High Street) turn off at Bully Hill crossroads, some 7 miles from Caistor, and head steeply downhill into Tealby.

Parking: Parking is available in the large pub car park for patrons of the King's Head but please let the landlord know you are leaving your car whilst walking. An alternative parking place is the car park at the Tennyson D'Enycourt Memorial Hall (village hall).

Length of the walk: 3½ miles. Map: OS Landranger 113 Grimsby & surrounding area (GR 157905).

THE WALK

1 Turn left out of the pub car park and keep to the right round the bend in the lane. At No. 31 on your right, turn right down the alleyway, labelled 'The Smootings', that quickly becomes a very attractive, stream-side path. Turn left uphill at the lane, go past the Memorial Hall on the right and cross

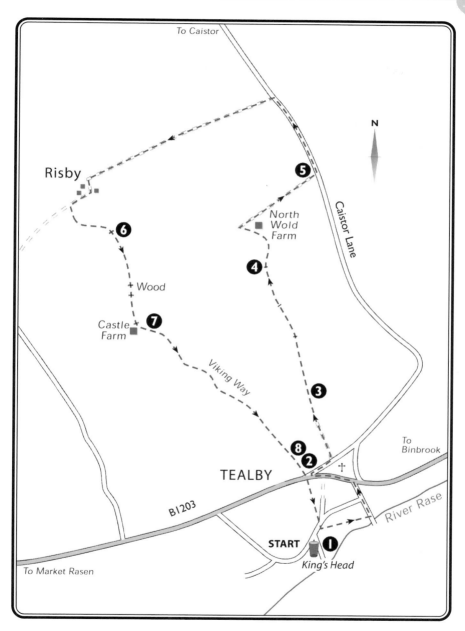

To Caistor

N

Risby

5

North
Wold
Farm

Caistor Lane

6

4

+ Wood

Castle
Farm

7

Viking Way

3

To
Binbrook

8
2

TEALBY

†

B1203

River Rase

To Market Rasen

START **1**

King's Head

the main road. Climb the steps on the left by the Caistor Lane road sign into the churchyard and follow the path round to the steps behind the church.

2 Turn right at the lane for 40 yards and then go left, uphill on the good signposted track. Take the blue metal fieldgate (waymarked) to the left of the house and, at the fence corner, walk ahead for 120 yards to the hedge 'corner'.

3 Go diagonally right across the grass field to the concealed stile in the dip at the far right-hand corner of the field. A wonderful panorama may be seen across Willingham Forest over on the left. Climb the stile and continue forward, with the hedge on your right over the next two stiles.

4 Then go diagonally across the field towards North Wold Farm, with an odd left turn in the path as you near the farm. Go through the wooden fieldgate into the farmyard and then turn right up the farm track to the road.

5 At the road, turn left for 350 yards along Caistor Lane and then go left up the signposted bridleway opposite the farm buildings. The bridleway is clearly marked through Risby farm buildings and after crossing the cattle grid just beyond the farmhouse, turn left through the gate and ahead along the grassy path that is the Viking Way, keeping the hedge and fence to your left.

6 At the metal fieldgate and stile, proceed diagonally left uphill to a stile in the corner of the field by the wood. Walk along the clear path by the wood edge and, at the end of the wood by Castle Farm, cross the stile.

7 Proceed left along the right-hand downward slope of the steep valley to the metal fieldgate and waymark in the extreme bottom right-hand corner of the field. Continue to follow the next field edge with the hedge on your right and some enormous boulders.

8 At the footpath signs, continue ahead past the bridge and stile on your right to another stile. Continue ahead along the next field, keeping the hedge on your right, to the gate in the field corner to the right of the house. Go over the main road and take the signposted footpath directly opposite and continue ahead through a kissing-gate, to follow the field edge, with a hedge now on your immediate left. At the stile and signpost by the lane, turn right to the King's Head car park.

The Wheatsheaf

A DELIGHTFULLY CONTRASTING TOWN AND COUNTRY WALK IN THIS 'JEWEL OF A TOWN', BELOVED BY JOHN BETJEMAN. THE LOVELY BEECH TREES IN THE WOODED GORGE OF HUBBARDS HILLS, THE SUPERB CROCKETED SPIRE OF ST JAMES'S CHURCH AND THE RIVER LUD, FLOWING THROUGH THIS ENCHANTED VALLEY ON ITS MEANDERING WAY TO THE SEA AT GRAINTHORPE HAVEN MAY ALL BE SEEN AND ENJOYED ON THIS ROUTE.

❖❖

The beautiful St James's church in Louth has a church spire that reaches 295 ft and is claimed to be the highest parish church spire in the land. After a bet made over a flagon of ale, a man named Anthony Fountain climbed to the top of the spire in 1771, and another, Benjamin Smith, after drinking ten pints of ale, in 1818, succeeded in tying a handkerchief round the iron which supports the weathercock. The original weathercock on the spire was fixed in 1515 amid great rejoicing for it was made from a copper basin which was part of the booty captured at Flodden Field from James IV of Scotland. John Betjeman wrote, 'This magnificent church is one of the last great medieval masterpieces'.

THE WHEATSHEAF is a charming hostelry which nestles almost at the foot of St James's church. Built as a coaching inn in 1625, it retains much of its original character. There are three low-beamed snug rooms, with an open fireplace in all the bars, photographs of old Louth on the walls and interesting clocks on display. In the yard behind the inn there are picnic tables and a red telephone box.

The pub offers a range of traditional fare and specials of the day every day except Sunday and the real ales include Flowers Original, Tipsy Toad, Black Sheep and guest ales.

Opening hours are 11 am to 3 pm and 5 pm to 11 pm, Monday to Friday; 11 am to 11 pm Saturday; and 12 noon to 4 pm and 7 pm to 10.30 pm on Sunday.

✆ 01507 606262.

How to get there: A route centre, Louth is 27 miles from Lincoln on the A157, 14 miles from Horncastle on the A153 and 15 miles from Market Rasen on the A631. It is also some 14 miles from the coast. The Wheatsheaf pub is in Westgate, at the foot of the church tower.

Parking: Customers may park in the pub car park but space is limited. There are plenty of municipal fee-paying car parks in the town or alternatively you could park at Hubbard's Hills car park and start the walk at point 3, visiting the Wheatsheaf en route.

Length of the walk: 3 miles. Map: OS Landranger 113 Grimsby and surrounding area (GR 326874).

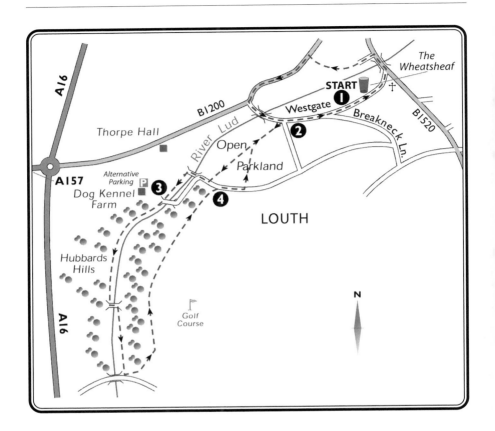

THE WALK

1 Turn left out of the car park and follow Westgate round to the left and then along the footway over the green on your left. Cross the bridge and turn left immediately, up to the attractive old graveyard where the gravestones are stacked five deep along the wall. Walk diagonally right across the open space to turn left at the road and go on to the Louth town sign. Turn left again towards Westgate, cross the bridge and the road to the white-painted fence and handgate at the beginning of Love Lane.

2 Walk along the tarmac path across the beautiful open parkland and turn right when you meet the lane. Continue along this lane for 100 yards and, just beyond the bend, cross over the river and walk forward, with the River Lud now on your left. Turn right on meeting the lane again and almost immediately left down the concrete slope by the toilets at the entrance to Hubbards Hills. Car parking and a restaurant are available here.

3 Walk forward through the valley, with the precipitous slope on your left, and continue on the good path, with the river at first on your left and then on your right. At the end of the park, turn left up the steep flight of steps and ten steps from the top, turn left again up some more steps to follow the high level path at the top of 'the cliff', with the beech trees clothing the steep slope on your left and a golf course on the right.

4 On coming down to the lane, continue forward, past the gate where you joined the route earlier and round the bend to a stile on the left. Climb the stile and walk across the parkland to the path leading to the white-painted handgate on Love Lane. Turn right along the main road as far as the junction with Breakneck Lane and then go left up Westgate back to the Wheatsheaf.

Spare some time to explore historic Louth if you can. At the side of the road on the bridge near the church are the remains of an old mill, with its mill race and a plaque indicating the height of the flood level in May, 1920, when the river rose 15 ft after a cloud burst and many people were drowned. The Greenwich Meridian passes through Louth and it is marked by a plaque on a shop in Eastgate and a metal strip on the pavement. By the church is a plaque commemorating the vicar Thomas Kendall, who was hanged at Tyburn for taking part in the Lincolnshire Rising in 1536.

The New Inn

A WALK OF GREAT CONTRASTS ACROSS FARMLAND, ALONG WIDE DYKES, OVER SANDHILLS AND THROUGH A NATURE RESERVE, WITH GLIMPSES OF THE SEA BEYOND THE SAMPHIRE MARSHES.

Saltfleet is an interesting little village that was once the principal port of the Roman province Flavia Caesarienses and the terminus of the great Fosse Way leading all the way to Exeter. In the days of sailing ships, there were numerous wrecks along this coast and old stories are still retold locally about ships being deliberatively wrecked off Saltfleet for salvage. All along the coast there were 'salvage sales', much of the timber being used in local building. One such sale was advertised to take place in the New Inn yard in May 1870, with salvage from the wreck of the *Hand of Providence*.

THE NEW INN used to be called the Dolphin and gave shelter to many sailors and merchants using the nearby little port of Saltfleet Haven. 'Traders of the night' were also constant callers, so that:

> Running round the woodlump, if you chance to find
> Little barrels, roped and tarred, all full of brandy wine
> Don't shout to come and look, nor take 'em for your play;
> Put the brushwood back again – they'll be gone next day.

The pub did have twelve letting bedrooms where the gentry used to come for a stay by the seaside. There is no accommodation available today but there is an extensive static caravan park with a children's play area immediately behind the inn. There is one enormous lounge, with a more intimate alcove by a front window, and a beer garden, with picnic tables on a grassed area at the front of the pub.

The New Inn is a freehouse serving a wide variety of beer, lagers and cider, plus chilled wine and a range of spirits. Good, plain food is served and may include home-made dishes, and vegetarians are catered for. Meals are served from March to October 12 noon to 2.30 pm and 5 pm to 7 pm Monday to Friday, Saturday 12 noon to 7 pm, and Sunday, 12 noon to 2.30 pm.

✆ 01507 338603.

How to get there: Saltfleet lies on the main A1031 between Grimsby and Mablethorpe. The New Inn is situated on the main road within yards of the prominent windmill.

Parking: There is ample parking by the New Inn but please park with care as it is a very busy entrance to the caravan park.

Length of the walk: 2¾ miles. Map: OS Landranger 113 Grimsby and surrounding area (GR 444938).

THE WALK

1 Turn right out of the New Inn along the main road down to the crossroads in 50 yards, marked 'The Hill'. Look first though at the signposted Chapel and Garden almost directly opposite the inn. This delightful, well-kept garden is dedicated to the people of the village who lost their lives in the floods of January 1953. Have a look at the inscription on the village pump to Trooper Freshney of the Imperial Light Horse and then turn left down Pump Lane, with the Crown Inn on your right. Follow this lane round to the left, with North Creek on your immediate right.

2 Cross the road and the bridge over North Creek to take the signposted diagonal path on the left that has been cleared across the arable field.

3 Turn left over the old stone bridge, cross the track and then go over the wooden bridge on the signposted path along the field edge, with the Mar Dyke Drain on your left. At the dyke junction with the Fleet Drain, cross the 52 ft bridge and continue ahead.

4 Towards the end of the field near the lane and Saltfleetby St Clement's old church, turn left over the splendid bridge and follow the path for a few yards over the stile to the road. Turn left at the lane and go straight across the main road past Sea View Farm.

5 Opposite the car park, turn left up the steep bank to follow the signposted path and then through the wooden fieldgate into the nature reserve, walking along the top of the sandhills, with the perimeter fence on your right. The protected ponds on your left are the breeding place of rare natterjack toads. At the corner of the fence alongside the ponds, don't follow the left-bearing path up the high dune

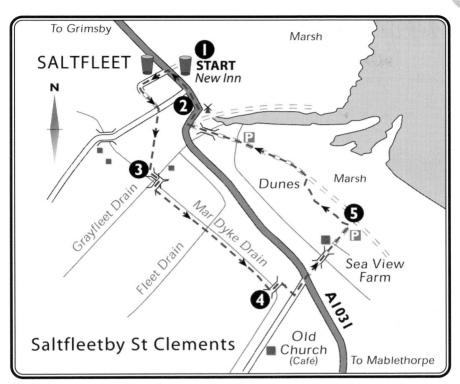

but bear right on a fainter path still keeping in line with the right-hand perimeter fence.

6 Go through the next gate, then turn immediately right and scramble down the short bank onto the good public track along the marsh edge. Turn left, walking towards the prominent landmark of the restored mill building. Walk straight across the old stone bridge above the Great Eau outfall and continue to the main road. Note here the signpost for 'Paradise'.

Walk back along the main road past the windmill to the New Inn.

The Jenny Wren

A N UNKNOWN AREA OF THE COUNTY FOR MANY PEOPLE, THIS IS A WALK FOR NATURE LOVERS. THE DELVINGS OR BORROW PITS CREATED DURING THE PROCESS OF BANK BUILDING ALONG THE RIVER EAU HAVE BECOME WILDLIFE HABITATS CONTAINING A VARIETY OF PLANTS SUCH AS WATER VIOLETS, SWEETGRASS, FLOWERING RUSH AND WATER SPEEDWELL. THEY ARE ALSO HOME FOR DRAGONFLIES, DARTERFLIES AND DAMSELFLIES WHICH MAY BE SEEN IN GREAT ABUNDANCE. THE REEDS PROVIDE COVER FOR NESTING BIRDS SUCH AS MALLARD, SWANS, COOT, TUFTED DUCK AND MOORHENS, AND THEY MAY ALL BE SEEN DURING THE WALK.

Susworth – *The Jenny Wren*

'Ea' means a stream. About 200 years ago, a prehistoric boat was found in these river pastures. In ancient times, the river Eau divided into three delta streams, Bellingfleet, Manfleet and the southern one Sennefleet, which originally meant 'the tidal inlet of the island at the junction of the tributary waters'. Sennafleet Lane is very old and this is indicated by the wide variety of trees in the hedgerows, including apples.

There are not many hamlets named after a particular person but Susworth is called after a man who, long ago, had a salmon fish farm or 'worth' here. Through the centuries his name has altered from Swyrkeswhod and Swerkeswat to Surrat, Surswath and finally to Susworth. There was once a wharf here at Susworth, by the side of the River Trent, and coal was unloaded for distribution around the district.

THE JENNY WREN is about 150 years old and must surely be one of the friendliest pubs in Lincolnshire. People come to Susworth to drive through the nearby woods and enjoy the quiet countryside but more particularly to experience the hospitality and welcome at the Jenny Wren. The river bank across the road from the pub is used as a beer garden and children are made particularly welcome. The Jenny Wren also offers superb accommodation at nearby Budleigh House, with all bedrooms having a riverside view.

It has always been important for the landlords to see that their customers get value for money and this is apparent in the quality of the beer and the food on offer. The exceptional bar menu ranges from fresh home-made soup through to the pub's speciality rack of lamb and local free-range pork dishes and the restaurant is very popular. Food is served from 12 noon to 2 pm and from 6 pm to 9 pm Tuesday to Friday, 12 noon to 9.30 pm Saturday, and 12 noon to 8 pm on Sunday. There is no food available on Monday.

How to get there: Turn westwards off the A159 Gainsborough to Scunthorpe road in Scotter village and drive 3 miles down the lane to Susworth.

Parking: Customers may leave their cars in the pub car park while on the walk. Alternatively, roadside parking may be available, with care, on the lane running parallel to the river.

Length of the walk: 4½ miles. Map: OS Landranger 112 Scunthorpe (GR 835021).

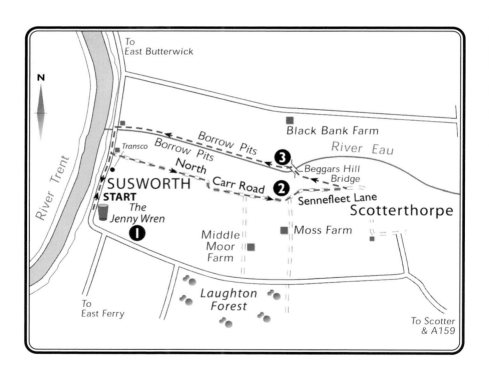

THE WALK

1 Turn right out of the Jenny Wren car park for about 1,000 yards, walking mainly along the River Trent embankment and then right up the track known as North Carr Road. Do not turn too early onto the farm track, but turn by the bungalow after Transco.

2 Follow this track, which becomes Sennefleet Lane, round the bend to the left where, after a couple of hundred yards, you will find a stile, gate and signpost to the left. Take this path to the splendid footbridge, christened by the children of the local primary school at the opening ceremony as 'Beggars Hill Bridge'.

3 Cross the bridge and turn left to walk along the bank, with the river Eau on your left. Continue all the way to the road, perhaps passing the old tramcar body on the right just before you reach the road. Turn left down the road back to your starting place.

The Ship Inn

A PLEASANT, PEACEFUL COUNTRYSIDE STROLL, ALMOST ENTIRELY ALONG GOOD TRACKS AND FIELD BOUNDARIES, WALKING THROUGH THE FLAT LANDS LEADING DOWN TO THE HUMBER ESTUARY SOME FIVE MILES AWAY. BARTON STREET ROMAN ROAD, THE 'CLIFF EDGE' OF THE WOLDS AND THE WOODS AT BRADLEY ARE IN VIEW AND THE MAGNIFICENT SIX-SAILED WINDMILL AT WALTHAM CAN BE SEEN ACROSS THE FIELDS. IT IS A WORKING LANDSCAPE AND BIG SKY COUNTRY THAT IS WELL WORTH EXPLORING.

❖❖

Like several villages in this area, Barnoldby once had strong Quaker connections and many Quaker families from hereabouts sailed from the nearby Immingham Creek in 1603 on their trip first to Plymouth, and then aboard the *Mayflower*, to land at Cape Cod to found the settlement that eventually became Massachusetts.

THE SHIP INN, over the years, has had some close connections with the sea and, indeed, the present landlords have their own fishing vessels and introduce many fine and varied fish dishes to their regular food menu. There is also a specials board which changes regularly and which contains many mouth-watering meals to suit all tastes. Freshly made sandwiches are also available whenever the kitchen is open. A good selection of beers, along with lagers, cider and wine is also on offer.

As well as a cosy 28-seater restaurant, the pub has a pleasant area to the rear laid out with tables and bedecked with hanging baskets and flower tubs in the summer months.

Opening hours all week are 12 noon to 3 pm and 6 pm to 11 pm (to 10.30 pm on Sunday).

✆ 01472 822308.

Website: www.The-shipinn.com

How to get there: Turn off the A46 Grimsby to Caistor road at the junction with the A18(T) road on Laceby roundabout and follow the A18 for 2½ miles before turning down into Barnoldby le Beck.

Parking: Customers may leave their cars in one of the two car parks at the Ship whilst they are walking, with the permission of the landlords. There is really no suitable alternative parking in the immediate vicinity although, by extending the route, it would be possible to park at Bradley Woods between points 2 and 3 of the walk.

Length of the walk: 4 miles. Map: OS Landranger 113 Grimsby and surrounding area (GR 235032).

THE WALK

1 Turn right out of the car park and immediately right again up Chapel Lane signposted 'bridleway' with a waymark for the Wanderlust Way (WW). Walk forward, with the church on your left and, after reading the inscription on the obelisk to the right, pass Glebe Farm Cottage with Waltham windmill coming into view.

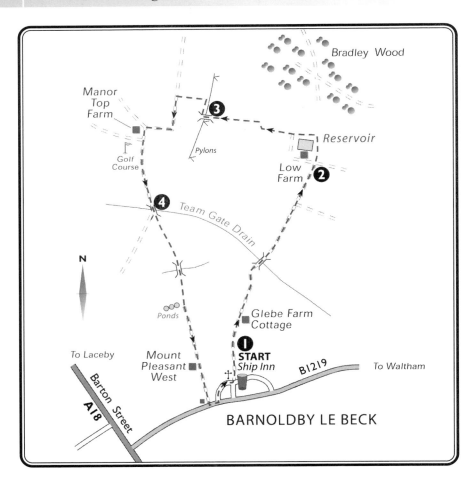

2 At Low Farm track junction continue to walk forward on the bridleway towards Bradley Wood, with a hedge on your left, for 200 yards.

Bradley Wood, with its picnic area and car parking, is owned by Grimsby Borough Council and you are free to wander around at will. A plaque explains that it is the start of the Wanderlust Way, a 20-mile circular route created as a tribute to Nev Cole, a well-loved local rambler.

However, to continue the walk, turn left off the bridleway onto a signposted footpath at the end of the reservoir (this path has been officially diverted but it may not be as indicated on your OS map). Follow the path, with the reservoir on your left at first. Continue on the track until it peters out, then walk ahead for 18 yards, turn right for another 18 yards, then by the solitary tree, turn left along the headland path until you reach the footbridge.

3 Cross the bridge and then turn right along the field edge for 180 yards, before turning left along the field boundary, with an old hedgeline and trees on your left. Go over the earth bridge and turn left along the good wide track towards Manor Top Farm, with its three green silos. Turn left at the farm and keep to the left track with a golf course on your immediate right. Follow this track until you reach Team Gate Drain.

4 Cross the bridge and proceed diagonally left on a (hopefully) defined path until you meet a footbridge over a side dyke. Walk forward from the bridge across the next field to the woods, then with the hedge on the left, follow the central path and track leading up to Mount Pleasant West. There are ponds and islands over on the right. Continue down this path to the road and then turn left to your starting place, after observing the date on the manor house across the road.

The Sheffield Arms

T HIS STROLL OFFERS WONDERFUL, TOTALLY UNEXPECTED
VIEWS ACROSS THE RIVER TRENT OVER THE GREEN ISLE OF
AXHOLME AND, IF CONDITIONS ARE SUITABLE, RIGHT ACROSS
YORKSHIRE TO YORK MINSTER.

At 200 ft above sea level, the 'upon' of Burton upon Stather
signifies that the village is situated above the River Trent and
not on it. This was the land of the Vikings and Stather is derived
from 'stoth' or 'staithe', meaning 'a landing place' in Old
Norse.

Important landowners in the area since the 16th century have
been the Sheffield family whose most illustrious member was

John Sheffield, third Earl of Mulgrave, who intrigued at court. Charles II made him a captain at sea and a colonel on land. King James made him Lord Chamberlain, King William made him Marquis of Normanby, and Queen Anne, Lord Privy Seal and Duke of Buckingham. The ancient ferry plying from Stather to Garthope was part of a route used by the king's messengers, who had to be given passage on demand. The ferry also carried passengers and was used for transporting sheep bound for Wakefield market. During the Second World War, units practised here with secret waterproofed tanks, preparing for the Rhine crossing.

THE SHEFFIELD ARMS was built in 1664 and at one time was known as the Black Bull, but changed its name out of respect for the Sheffield family. This friendly inn is an imposing building right at the end of the high street, adjacent to the church, and has always been important to the prosperity of the village. It has been carefully refurbished and now the bars have all the comfort you could ask for, but have lost none of their old appeal. An L-shaped bar serves the old, beamed lounge, with its panelling and comfortable settle seating. There are brasses and paintings decorating the walls and an interesting map of the area.

The inn serves a range of beers and lagers, including premium grades. There is also a wide variety of meals available both lunchtime and evening in the bar and lounge and a separate 40-seater restaurant.

Opening times are 11.30 am to 11 pm Monday to Saturday, and 12 noon to 3 pm and 7 pm to 10.30 pm on Sunday, ✆ 01724 720269.

How to get there: Burton upon Stather is 5 miles north of Scunthorpe on the B1340, signposted as a scenic route. Alternatively, turn off the A1077 road at Winterton, going to Thealby and then on to Burton upon Stather.

Parking: Customers may park at the pub while they are doing the walk. There is no other suitable parking available in the immediate vicinity but it would be possible to park at the picnic stop at point 5 of the route and visit the pub en route.

Length of the walk: 3 miles. Map: OS Landranger 112 Scunthorpe (GR 870179).

THE WALK

1 From the car park, walk down the narrow passage to the left of the pub into Main Street and continue down the road, with the post office on your right. At the bend, leave Main Street to follow the signposted, tarmac footpath on the right.

2 After 35 yards, where the tarmac path turns left to the road, continue ahead on the waymarked grass footpath to the gap and stile. Then bear right and turn left down the steps and continue downhill to the gate in the bottom right-hand corner of the field.

3 Through the gate, head up the lane, leaving the sewage plant behind you.

4 About 175 yards past the farmhouse on your left, turn left down a good track**, with a large fishing pond on your left. Turn right upon reaching the river bank, along the raised flood control embankment, past the navigation beacon.

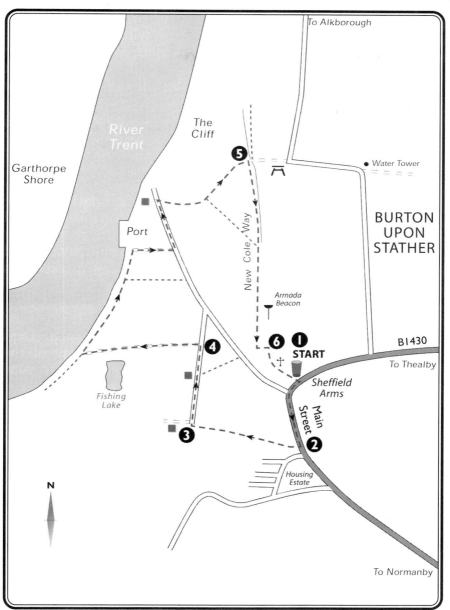

Upon reaching the port complex, turn right down a clear path to the road. Turn left at the road, with the Ferry House Inn and Kings Ferry House on your left, and then right up the signposted path, going steeply uphill. Ignore the first footpath on the right halfway up the hill and proceed to the top.

**(If the track is not available, then continue ahead along Chafer Lane. Turn left at the road, left again down Old Row (footpath) to the river bank and turn right to resume your route.)

5) Turn right by the footbridge leading to the car park, with the drain on your left. Walk on past the Armada Beacon and turn left up the narrow path to the churchyard, shortly after passing the kissing-gate. To the west of the churchyard wall is the site of the ancient market. A Tuesday market was chartered by the Earl of Lancaster in 1315.

6) Turn into the churchyard and walk past the 13th-century, much restored church to the car park at the Sheffield Arms on your left. Have a look at the lovely doorway of the church and, if it is open, do take time to go inside to view the many monuments to the Sheffield family.

BARROW HAVEN

The Haven Inn

A WALK FOR BIRD LOVERS, FOR THIS STROLL EXPLORES A REMOTE NATURE RESERVE ON THE HUMBER BANK, WITH A SPLENDID VIEW UPSTREAM OF THE WORLD-RENOWNED BRIDGE THAT HAS A BEAUTY ALL OF ITS OWN. THE GREYLAG GOOSE, RUDDY DUCK, OR POSSIBLY THE SPARROWHAWK, MAY BE SEEN, WHILE CANADA GEESE, COLLARED DOVES AND LESSER WHITETHROATS HAVE INCREASED IN THESE OLD CLAY PIT RESERVES.

Barrow Haven is an ancient place, for the green mounds known as the Castles, on a good strategic position by the beck, are the extensive remains of a great Saxon or Danish earthwork, covering eight acres. Just four miles away, at the hamlet of Burnham, legend cites the historically important Battle of Brunanburh, where King Athelstan routed the enemies of Wessex, killing five kings and establishing the unity of England. Today, though, Barrow Haven is a small port dealing mainly in Scandinavian timber, with an odd little railway station on a branch line that actually still functions.

THE HAVEN INN was built in the 1740s and, until the late 1800s, offered accommodation and hospitality to passengers to and from the Humber ferry, sailing at that time from Barrow Haven. This comfortable pub is a freehouse, with well-kept Worthington and Black Sheep beers, Woodpecker cider and lagers. The extensive menu offers excellent home-cooked meals from a traditional Sunday carvery to lasagne, vegetarian options and a variety of pies. Sandwiches are also available. Reduced rates apply to senior citizens and children.

The pub has a large games room, with a dartboard and pool table, and there is a pleasant restaurant. Nine en suite rooms are available for overnight accommodation.

Opening hours are 12 noon to 11 pm (to 12 midnight on Saturday and to 10.30 pm on Sunday).

☎ 01469 530247.

How to get there: Turn off the A1077 Barton-upon-Humber to Barrow upon Humber road at a very sharp, right-angled bend, where it is signposted 'Barrow Haven'. The pub is almost 1 mile down this lane.

Parking: Customers may leave their cars at the Haven, whilst they are walking, or it would be possible to park on the roadside near the railway crossing, north of the inn.

Length of the walk: 2 miles. Map: OS Landranger 112 Scunthorpe (GR 062230).

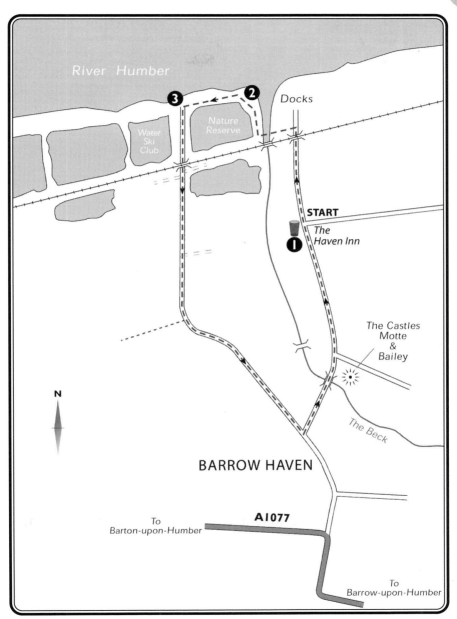

River Humber

Docks

3

2

Water
Ski
Club

Nature
Reserve

START

The
Haven Inn

1

The Castles
Motte
&
Bailey

N

The Beck

BARROW HAVEN

A1077

To
Barton-upon-Humber

To
Barrow-upon-Humber

THE WALK

1 Turn left out of the inn car park to walk along the road for 700 yards, with the drain embankment on your left. Turn left at the railway bridge over the tidal drain and immediately right into Barrow Haven Reedbed Nature Reserve. The steps on the left of the path lead down to a birdwatching hide that you may wish to explore but it is a cul-de-sac.

2 Follow the Humber bank to just before the metal gate and ski club caravan park. Then turn left down the track away from the bank. (The exact status of this well-used short stretch of track to the railway has not been established. If its use should change, then an alternative enjoyable route is available along the Humber Bank and back.)

3 Follow this good track, with the water ski club on your right and an extensive reedbed on the left. Go through the handgate and the two railway gates at the level crossing and continue down the long straight section of West Marsh Lane to eventually follow the lane round the bend to the left, turning sharp left towards the bridge over the beck, and past the old mill back to the Haven Inn.

The Black Bull

E AST HALTON IS A LITTLE VILLAGE OF THE BYWAYS, ONLY A COUPLE OF MILES FROM THE HUMBER. THIS PLEASANT WALK PASSES THE FINE REMAINS OF THORNTON ABBEY ON EAST HALTON BECK.

Thornton Abbey was founded by the Lord of Holderness in 1139 and, after the Dissolution of the Monasteries, Henry VIII held his court there for three days in 1541. It once covered 100 acres and was surrounded by a wall and a moat, the remains of which bear testimony to its former magnificence. Today, the splendid gatehouse, built of stone and brick, and standing 50 ft high, provides an obvious photographic souvenir.

THE BLACK BULL is a friendly local pub, much frequented by members of the farming community. It has a U-shaped bar, with a games annexe that includes a pool table and a dartboard. There is a very comfortable lounge bar at the rear, with plush seating, brown décor and old variety act prints on the wall. There are restaurant facilities for up to fifty people and a pleasant garden area for children outside.

The menu is extensive, with weekly specials, vegetarian options and a complete change of fare every two months. A children's menu is also available. This is a Marston's house, serving real ales, and an extensive range of beers, including Creamy Bitter, Carling, Foster's and Guinness. There are also two to four guest ales and bottled beers.

The opening times are 12 noon to 11 pm Monday to Saturday, and 12 noon to 10.30 pm on Sunday.
☎ 01469 540207.

How to get there: From the A160, which runs from the A180, Brigg to Grimsby road, turn north at South Killingholme and go through North Killingholme to East Halton.

Parking: Customers may park in the Black Bull car park. There is alternative roadside parking in the immediate vicinity.

Length of the walk: 4¼ miles. Map: OS Landranger 113 Grimsby and surrounding area (GR 139195)

THE WALK

1. Turn right out of the pub car park and walk along the road for 350 yards, then right down the signposted farm track almost opposite Swinster Lane. Follow this clear track and,

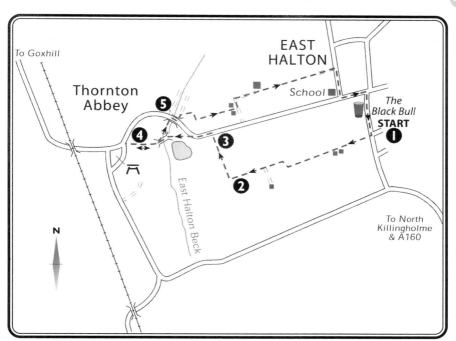

where it turns left to the farm, continue ahead along the headland path.

2. On reaching the path junction by the hedge, go through the wooden fieldgate and turn right along the rutted track, with the hedge on your right and the abbey over on your left across the field.

3. Turn left at the road and, at the sharp bend, turn left at the start of the metal crash barrier, through the handgate. Facing the abbey across the pond, turn a quarter right across the field, keeping the pond to your left, to the splendid bridge with a stile. Cross the bridge and walk a quarter left to a smaller second footbridge. Go up the steps and turn left to go through a kissing gate. Turn immediately

right alongside the fence and hedge, keeping it on your right (although the definitive map shows the path on the other side of the hedge). In the corner, go through another kissing gate, then turn left. Continue forward, down the steps, over the bridge and through another gate to the road.

4   Turn left at the road to the abbey, where there is a picnic place outside which would be a good apple stop.

Thornton Abbey (English Heritage) is open daily from 1st April to 30th September (10 am to 6 pm) and during the rest of the year at weekends only (10 am to 4 pm). There is an admission charge.

5   After viewing (and photographing) the abbey, retrace your steps from the picnic site as far as the crash barrier at the bend in the road. Cross the road with care and turn left along it. Go over the road bridge and turn right down a track with East Halton beck on your right.

Cross the footbridge over the beck after a few yards, then walk slightly left for 30 yards and over the next wooden bridge. Walk half left over the first field, aiming for the centre of a large barn and the fence in the foreground. Go over the stile in the fence and turn right for 10 yards, then turn left, resuming your direction up the rise on the defined path, now heading for the right-hand edge of the barn. *(Note: The definitive line of the path to the barn is shown as running along the left-hand edge of the barn but the route described is the one provided on the ground as the proposed alternative.)* On reaching the barn, continue ahead to the track, turn left, then right along the straight green lane, which leads you past a farmhouse to the road. Turn right at the road and, upon reaching the junction with the main road, with the school on your right, turn left up the main road and then right at the road junction, back to the Black Bull.